Shi Ma' (My moms)

Vivian Badoni

Illustrations by Melissa Smith and Vivian Badoni

Presentation by *BookLeaf Publishing*

Web: www.bookleafpub.com

E-mail: info@bookleafpub.com

ISBN: 9789358367973

First edition 2023

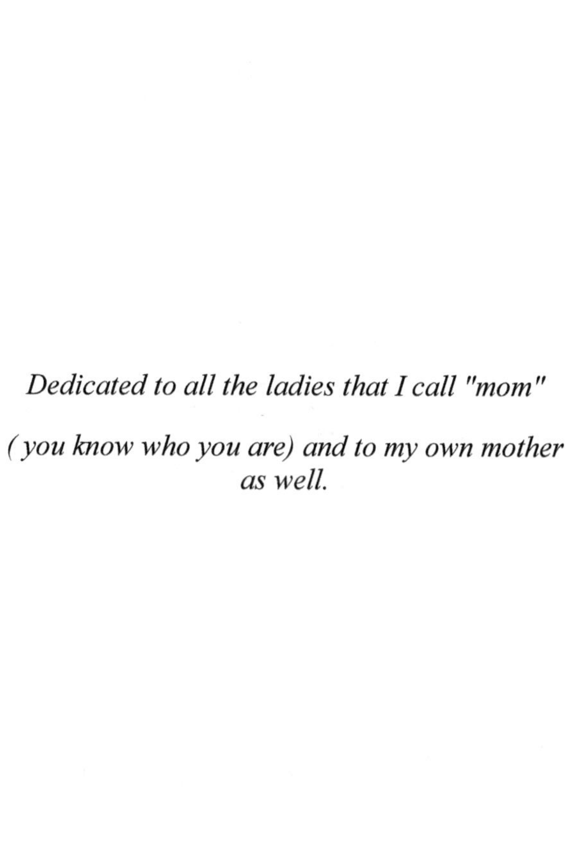

Dedicated to all the ladies that I call "mom"

(you know who you are) and to my own mother
as well.

Learning How to Braid

For as long as I can remember,
my mom braided my hair,

Her fingers take my hair in three parts
at the top of my head, she starts
with a glass full of water.

In that I sat, shifting to the right
then to the left;
she dips her fingers in a cup of water
and continues.

10 years later I stare at my own eyes:
"Mom was right."
I grab my hair,
look at the comb.
"Should've learned. . ."
My hands reach for my phone, my fingers glide
as they type
"How to braid your own hair"

"One day you will have to learn this."
I say nothing,

In those days I wasn't into braids.
I thought of it being too girly

That went with bright pink dresses
Tight skin tights that matched the hair ties.

"I don't like braids." I pouted.
Arms crossed and eyes wandering.
Impatient.

Three sections are what I remembered:
One over the other and I repeat,
My first braid was loose and messy.
I lowered my head.
My first try
Hanging down my back.
Proud that I did it, I stood straight.

Next time:
I took the three sections:
Tipping my head back to help me
With the weaving.
One over the other
I lay over with my fingers tightened as I go.
Careful not to let any strands free or left out.
I continue until my hair runs out.
I get up with a better braid….

Better than the last, the first messy braid.

My lips slip into a smile
"I finally learned how to braid."

Phyllis

Persistent in
Her ways, my mom
Yields to no one. She
Lovingly helped us
Like any mother, she
Inspired us to
Stay focused on our dreams.

Because . . .

Bad things can happen
And she reminded us to kneel
Down & pray to the
One above for strength but to
Never give up.
I will always look up to her for that.

Her Favorite Things

Purple
Any shade of purple
will have her glee like a little
girl again.
As long as I can remember
she always wore purple.

Butterflies
The Moths opposite cousin.
She adored the unique

symmetrical patterns.
Anything with Butterflies
sends her flying and fluttering
with happiness.

Flamingos
Standing on one leg
not losing balance
in the still lakes
that reflect
the bright pink feathers.
They would always catch her attention,
she would wish that she could pet them.

Butterfingers
The candy of The Simpsons
The famous saying
"Don't lay a finger on my Butterfinger."
She would laugh at the commercials
then crave that buttery crunch.
Her favorite of favorites.

Butter Pecan Ice cream
The pecans.
The buttery flavor
in
the ice cream
brought out the kid in her.
Her smile became 10yrs younger.

With each bite, her eyes once again twinkled.

Most of all
Her kids
are her favorite,
nieces and nephews,
and grandkids.
She treasures each and every one of them.

Making Dough

"You need to learn to make dough."
She would say this
as she gathered the needed ingredients and
supplies.
Flour
Salt
Baking powder and
Lukewarm water.

"This is how you make dough."
Adding flour by handfuls to a bowl,
then palm fulls of baking powder,
keeping it a 1:1 ratio,
then a pinch of salt.

Her hand carefully sifted
and mixed the ingredients together,
making sure they're well combined.

Once mixed,
she heads to the sink,
toggles with the facet
until she gets the desired temperature.
Adding the water little by little,
with her free hand, she begins

to mix the ingredients,
all the while making sure it's forming a ball.

Turning the bowl,
adding water,
combining flour mix and water,
until all the flour is gone
and all that's left is a ball of dough.

"Clean your hands.
Cover your dough to let it rest."
She takes a plate and covers the dough.

My Mother's Prayer

"Dear Lord in Heaven,
Please watch over my daughter
and her boyfriend, Trenton,
as they go to work.

Please Lord,
Give them the strength
to get through the day
and
to face the battles that they may face today.

Be there for them when they need it.
Protect them from things that may want to harm
them.
I thank you, Lord, for giving us another day to
live.
We thank you, Lord, for all that you provide us.
Thank you.
Amen."

Snacks of Affection

Fruit
Life's natural source of endorphins.
She hands me a bowl of assorted fruit

Food is her love language.

Oreos
Black and white sandwich cookies,
cream-filled and delicious with milk.
(Even though I'm lactose intolerant).
She knows that's my favorite.

Sour and gummy candies.
Small boxes of candy
one dollar each
left on the dining table.
No note, but
the lingering care and affection from her.

Each snack she chooses
she chooses carefully.
Thinking, wondering
if I am still the same girl who loves each of
those.

Small yet Strong

Her hair falls to her frail shoulders
in natural streaks of grey and white.
She complains of having too many greys
and heeds her sister's words about using coconut
oil.

Wrinkles start to show on her
suntanned hands
and painted nails.

Her dark chocolate eyes
reflect mine in turn as
she smiles in joy
just to see me emerge
from my cave of isolation.

She's small and frail-looking
as she navigates around the apartment.
Her will,
her faith,
and her love
are strong.

Strong as the bunk bed
that holds a family of 3 at night.

Her faith is like spider webs
holding the family together
as she prays each morning and night.

Her love is like Venus as it rises each morning
and when it greets the evening.

With Care

15

With care
she holds
my hands in hers
as a smile slowly appears
accompanied by a pair of crow's feet.
She recites a prayer
to give me strength for a new day,
and to keep me safe.

With care
her arms wrap around me
as she whispers,
"I love you."
and
"Have a good day at work."

Always with care
she'll embrace me
and lets me go
with a soft smile
that warms my heart.

With care
I will remember these actions for a lifetime.

I Listen

Every day she smiles
with a cup of decaf
"Yá'át'ééh abíní." (Good morning)

She'll talk about the days
of black and white photos
when Polaroid pictures were still new.
For her in those days,
the smiles came by a dozen.

She would switch to
family issues:
of sickness and
deaths from covid or natural.
Her amber eyes droop to her mug
as her wrinkled hands tighten.

She thinks I don't listen to her.

But her voice is
shaking with each word.
She continues,
and forces a smile,
"I love you che'e (daughter)"

She waits.

"I love you too Mom"
Her smile turns genuine.
Her shoulders drop slightly,
her grip loosens on the cup.
"God loves you too."

I nod.

She doesn't think I listen.
Her words at times
sting like a wasp
as she leaves an awkward silence.

Her hair is loose
and falls about her oval-tanned face,
with strands of silver and grey.
She's still holding her decaf coffee,
her gaze is unfazed
as she looks into my eyes
searching and waiting for something.
As if waking up, her creamed coffee eyes
light up, "My coffee, I better drink it."

She turns to leave,
and her footsteps echo
"I love you."

My Mom Prays

She prays in bed
as she's wrapped
in a blanket late at night
waiting for God to lull her to sleep.

My mom prays
as she greets the dawn,
rising to get ready for the day,
thanking Him for being alive
and to be able
to see her kids again.

My mom whispers words
of appreciation
before she breaks bread,
before she takes a sip of tea.
She tells Him,
she is grateful for having food.

She'll take our hands
and close her eyes.
She'll start to pray
asking the Lord to watch over us,
to take care of us
and once again

thanking Him for letting us have jobs.

My Mom will always pray.

A Lesson Learned

She would say "Nida!" (Sit Down).
Her eyes melted into pools of chocolate.
As her voice softened like butter.
Then she would begin:

"Nik'adą́ą́," (Some time ago)
Our eyes followed her gesture.
Her hands were shaped like a rainbow.
And led us back to the past:

"When I was small,
Just a child around your age.
I would herd sheep, sometimes by myself.
But mostly with your zhe'eh yaazhi (uncle),
Lee."

I would turn in my spot as if to see if said Uncle
was behind me.
She continued,
"We would take the sand rocks and shape them
into toys."
"Toys?"
"You know. Like cars, chairs, people, and tables.
And we would just play with these toys as the
sheep camp."

Her lips curved into a smile.
I felt a tug at my heart. My mom missed those
days.
"Sometimes we would get caught up in playing.
And the sheep would run off on us…"

She paused.
"We ran after them. Yelling at them to stop.
We would scream 'Dibe!' and 'Heeeey!'
They would just keep walking like they didn't
hear us.
The dogs ran ahead as they barked at the sheep.
We kept running.
We forgot our toys."

A laugh escaped me as I pictured it.
My mom, my uncle.
Two native kids in jeans and 70's shirts
Running after the clouds of wool and hooves
With arms frantically waving in the air.
All the while trying not to step into the hiding
cactus.

My mom's eyes thinned to a slit
as she cracked up with me.

"We ran 'cause we didn't want to get in trouble,
you know?"
I nodded, with hiccups of laughter.

"Your great grandma wasn't one to mess with."
"Anyways we caught up and stopped them.
So honey, my che'e (daughter),
never play with toys when you herd sheep."
Again we fell into a fit of giggles.
A fine lesson learned.

Artemis

Dedicated to the Greek Goddess Artemis

In the forest,
there is a soul,
a calm, caring presence that envelopes me.
I call her mother.
She is my mother
when my mom wasn't there.

In her shades of green
and earth tones,
she sent Does to guide me.

On days of unbearable grief,
I heard her call
to walk the trails of her creatures.
I felt her embrace in the wind
when I sat and cried
asking "why"
to a boulder that supported me.

To me, she is my mother.
She was there as the moon
when I felt alone in depression.
Urging me to go on and take strength
from her silver light.
To learn from her cycles,
everything has a turn,
everything will come full circle.

That is why I call her mom,
which is why I heed her call.
She is the path I know
that I can't get lost on.

She is Artemis.
Goddess of the Hunt.

Protector of girls, young women, and women.
Goddess of chastity and childbirth.
She is what I call mom.

Thinking of Home

Dedicated to my late maternal grandma, Jennie
Blake.

When I think of "Home"
My masani's (maternal grandma's) home

I see a stretched canvas of blue
With sponge-painted clouds
And streaks of
Sunlight.

Imagine an endless black sky
embedded with multicolored gems
as they sparkle off the
Moon's pseudo light.

I stand in that open space
of pop-up brushes,
and wild aqua green sage
That mimics the look of sheep,
Who are just as fluffy and white
like those cotton candy clouds
With scattered cedar and juniper trees.

When I think of home
I can cry as she wraps
me in her frail arms of velvet,
And whispers, "Shí che'e, welcome home."

That's when I say to myself,
"I'm home again."

My Spanish Mom

Dedicated to Erika R.

She came unexpectedly.
Like a breeze that decided to stay,
To keep you cool during the summer.

She became the friend
Who showed up
When it seemed like the world was against you.

She was the shoulder
For me to cry on.
That same shoulder
was there when I needed to vent.

As months went by,
Our friendship deepened.

Soon, I looked for her
Like a lost toddler
With many tears
Made from life's walls
Of discouragement
And judgment.

When life growled
And threatened to eat me alive,
I ran to her
Like a baby animal
To its mother.

She stood in front of me,
Arms at the ready
With words
To shield me from harm's way.

When we parted,
I still call her a friend,
But in my heart
She is my Spanish mom.

Second Mom

Dedicated to Roberta G.

The Native Americans have family everywhere.
Brothers
Sisters
Moms
Dads
Uncles, etc.

For that, we are to take care of each other.

Roberta was that.
She's my 2nd mom.

She saw me as I was.
Took me in like mother nature does.
Didn't question my thoughts,
But made sure I was still there
Emotionally
And mentally.

On my birthday
There was always a cake
With a smile
And the song to follow.

She's my 2nd mom.
She made sure
My homework was done
And I went to school.

She took me in when no one else would.
Made me feel like me.
For that, I am thankful to her.

She stood up for me.
I learned that from her.
I learned to speak up.
To Stand up.
To fight.

She's my 2nd mom.

Ellouise

Dedicated to my late aunt, Ellouise H.

Words are not enough to describe her love.

She warmed the room with her presence,
To be cliché,
She was like the sun to me.

Her hug was the fireplace
On a cold winter's night.

Her smile and her laugh
Brought joy
Like Christmas day
And birthdays:
A never-ending gift.

She was the epitome
Of what you call unconditional love,
Because her love was Mobius strip.
Her love knew no bounds and was infinite.

It was deeper than space.
Brighter than the full moon at night.

She was my mom and my aunt.

I will always love her.

To the Moms

You are everything.
You are everyone.

We take you for granted.
As we sneak out of the house
To get away from the warnings
We call as nagging.

We put you on silent
When your ringtone comes on,

Only to be scolded later
For forgetting to defrost things for dinner.

We toss aside the advice
You give for free.
And think your wisdom is ancient and useless.
Only wishing later we could hear it again.

We yearn to get away,
But time draws us back to you.

To replay all the times
We took your time for granted.
We know now that your advice is golden.
Your naggings are warnings.
Your teachings are more than learned.

Thank you, mothers.
For all you do.

Mom's Hug

(A haiku)

A mother's hug is
A warm blanket in the night
That is soft and warm.

M.O.T.H.E.R

Maternally love that lasts
On forever.
This kind of love
Has been
Embedded into our lives.
Red and raw is their love.

Maternal Instincts

(a Haiku)

A fighting spirit
That knows no boundaries
To protect her young.

She is Mom

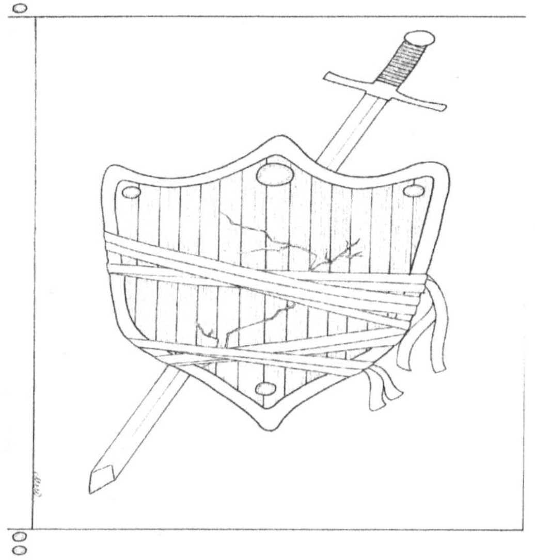

She is a sweet lullaby in the night
When all is lost.

She is the hammer to the nail
When lines have been crossed
And to put you in your place.

She is the bandaid
To your scarred heart
When no one can heal
What has hurt you.

She is your shield when
The world is against you
And she is your sword when
You need strength.

She is just that.
A heroine to look up to.
She is "mom".

9 789358 367973